T0195802

BROKENNESS
and
NEW
BEGINNINGS

A Story of Hope for Those Facing
Separation and Divorce

FRANCIS P. DELELLIS

WESTBOW
PRESS®
A DIVISION OF THOMAS NELSON
& ZONDERVAN

WestBow Press books may be ordered through
booksellers or by contacting:

WestBow Press
A Division of Thomas Nelson & Zondervan
1663 Liberty Drive
Bloomington, IN 47403
www.westbowpress.com
844-714-3454

Scripture quotations are taken from the Holy Bible, New International
Version®, NIV®. Copyright © 1973, 1978, 1984 by Biblica, Inc.™
Used by permission of Zondervan. All rights reserved worldwide.

ISBN: 978-1-6642-9788-3 (sc)
ISBN: 978-1-6642-9790-6 (e)

Library of Congress Control Number: 2023907051

Print information available on the last page.

WestBow Press rev. date: 6/20/2023

Contents

Epigraph

Psalms 30:2

New International Version

2 Lord my God, I called to you for
help, and you healed me.

Introduction

Life can change in an instant. Happiness becomes sadness. Hope becomes hopelessness. Joy becomes pain, and for some, 'til-death-do-us-part becomes separation and divorce. Where does one turn when they are in the midst of marital crisis and decline? How does one overcome the evil of fear, uncertainty, and doubt as it consumes every aspect of daily life?

When I experienced marital crisis, I didn't know what the future had in store for me. My faith was weak. My work life was in shambles. I scrambled for any glimmer of hope I could find. I didn't know where to turn to get help, and the embarrassment of the possibility of divorce caused me to create a façade of happiness, which only prevented those with a willingness to help realize I needed them to do so.

Brokenness and New Beginnings provides a message of hope to anyone who feels like their life is crumbling in front of their eyes. It is steady ground upon which to stand so they may begin the process of healing the wounds caused by separation and the possibility of divorce.

Preface

I am not a doctor or a psychiatrist. I am not a psychologist or a sociologist. I am not a theologian or a religious educator. I am not a professional writer or a master storyteller. I am simply a humbled man who has survived separation and divorce, and I write to you today to offer you a story of hope—my story.

I was sitting at my kitchen table. My once-bustling home was now an empty house, and I was very much alone. I did not want to be alone, but I was, and I was miserable. I was less than a month into my separation and trying to adapt to my new reality. I was filled with gut-wrenching emotions and pain. I could barely eat or sleep. I was struck by the realization that I was not the only one in the world who was hurting from separation and divorce or the possibility of that reality. I decided at that moment that I would write about my experience with the hope of one day helping others. I didn't even know if I'd survive my own ordeal, but I vowed I'd share my story. I didn't begin writing until two years later, but I remember that day as if it were yesterday. I sat in utter disbelief of my reality. My existence seemed surreal.

I ended up in my position after a whirlwind of activity. I was happy one day, and literally the next, my wife and I were in crisis. After a week of me wondering what was wrong, my wife stated she wanted to separate. Approximately a month after that dreadful day, on September 22, she had the separation agreement drafted, and it was ready for our signatures. On September 27, she moved out of our home. Two days later, our children began their new life of switching between their parents' respective houses. The chaotic frenzy of activity left me feeling dazed by the ambush.

My ex-wife and I remain civil toward each other. That was a decision we made early in our separation for the sake of our children. I was brokenhearted by my situation, but I was blessed with the realization that fighting through the divorce process would only harm our children. The grief I experienced through the process was unbearable, and for a few months I was actually in denial that my marriage would fail. Unfortunately, divorce would be my eventual reality.

This story is of my journey. I hope you read it and, if you can relate to it, that you are able to find solace in the fact that you too can make it through to the other side. I want to walk with you through your journey, but the only way I know how to do that is to share my story and experiences with you. Regardless of the outcome you face, I assure you our Lord Jesus Christ has wonderful things in store for you. You may not understand this right now, but I assure you it can be your reality too. I encourage you to draw from my experience and my strength. I want you to believe your life, with all its pain and uncertainty, can change for the better. It is my sincere hope that my experience and the insight I share here somehow helps you get through this challenging time in your life. I hope, by sharing my experience, you will discover insights of your own. If you do, then I will consider all that I went through to be worth it in the end.

Chapter 1

Soul Shock

Devil – 1; Me – 0. That was the score back in September. Today that is no longer the score. I have blown the game wide open. I'm still in extreme danger and vulnerable, but I have made significant advances and keep tallying up the points in this game we call life.

The changes that took place in my life were significant. I didn't know what hit me. Above all, I want you to know peace and happiness returned to my life. I also want to reassure you they can return to your life too. There will be some tough choices you will have to make, but peace and happiness can be your reality once again; both are a choice. I had to learn to choose peace and happiness while in despair and sorrow.

Perhaps you think I don't know the depth of your misery and despair. The fact that I can speak of peace and happiness may be enough to discredit me to somebody experiencing a psychic tsunami. You are right. I don't know where you are in your journey, not exactly, but I can tell you where I've been.

In the initial stages of the separation process, I questioned my ability to survive the destruction of life as I'd come to know it. My entire reality was destroyed by mere separation, let alone the divorce to follow. How can I talk about happiness at this time? I simply want to encourage you to keep hope alive. You ache and despair because something priceless and beautiful has been lost. The intensity of your pain is born in the reality that something that meant so much is gone forever—yet you continue to feel it.

It is in that reality that hope can be fostered. I'm talking about hope in the reality that you will not merely survive this ordeal but also grow as a result. Perhaps all you want to do right now is cry. Go ahead. It's healthy. I encourage you to cry. Crying helped me heal. I understand the pain and anxiety associated with separation and divorce can consume your life. Today is a new day. Today is your day. Today is the beginning of your *new* journey. You may fear and dread what is to come, but I assure you peace and happiness are available if you will make the conscious decision to allow them to be your companions through this journey. I'm confident you will find them.

My initial soul shock came during one of our marriage-counseling sessions. The words will be forever burned in my mind. I sat on one end of the couch, and my wife sat on the other. "I'm done. It's over. I'm through," she said. I couldn't believe the words I was hearing. I was in such denial that I actually said, "No, it isn't over." I was wrong, and she was right; it was the beginning of the end. I could barely breathe.

My stomach was in my throat as I sat on that couch trying to understand what was happening to me. I felt like I had to fix this mess, but I didn't know how. Our counselor suggested going to a marriage workshop as a last-ditch effort to save the marriage.

Two weeks later, we were on our way to Atlanta for the weekend event. At that event, I realized my wife didn't want to revive the relationship but wanted to help me recognize our marriage was over. It was the most horrible time of my life. It was at that event I actually had to tell her I was setting her free—free from me.

Only God knows the pain I felt. I shook uncontrollably. I wanted to throw up. Perhaps you can relate to these feelings. It was as though evil raised up from the earth, grabbed me, and then slammed me violently against the ground. I stopped eating. I couldn't imagine what was happening to me. I was in a state of shock—a shock directly to my soul.

I felt evil won that day. My heart was torn out and smashed into a million pieces. My already-weakened faith was blown away. I was living in a world of darkness, despair, pain, and broken dreams. Again, Devil – 1; Me – 0.

How did you feel when you learned your marriage was over? Was your experience like mine? Perhaps yours was even worse. Perhaps you are right in the midst of your own soul shock as you read these words and hope to salvage your marriage. Wherever you are in your marriage situation, I want you to take a few deep breaths and try to relax—if only for a minute. Close your eyes and repeat these words: "Lord God, help me, please." Do it now. Repeat it. Repeat it over and over. These simple words will change your life. They changed mine. "Lord God, help me, please."

God did help me through the uncharted chasms of despair and brokenness. I was helplessly lost. I felt forsaken, abandoned, and cast out. I felt lonely and forgotten, but God sustained me through all of it.

After that Atlanta weekend event, I came home and tried to act as though I was totally healthy and happy. In reality, I was a walking disaster. I was not eating. I was not sleeping. I could barely concentrate on my work, and I could barely face the people I knew because I feared they would detect something was wrong with me. I didn't know how to be anything other than a loving husband, father, and family man. It was my entire identity, and suddenly, I was living as an impostor.

At one point, work ruled my life. Two days after my wife and I physically separated, life kicked me once again while I was down. I simply couldn't believe what was happening to me. My life turned upside down in a flash. The company I worked for collapsed and was taken over by a rival. All I had accomplished and all I was recognized for were worthless and no longer important. There were days, nights, and weekends I dedicated my time to my work. Amazing. I thought I was making a good living, but God helped me—very quickly, mind you— realize people are much more important than work ever should have been.

I eventually made the decision to tell my

coworkers and my boss I was going through a divorce. I was nervous at first. I thought they would view me as a failure in life. In reality, I was confronted with genuine concern and support. I pray you are met with the same when you decide to open your heart to those around you. Understand that your experience may differ from mine, but my reality demonstrated the genuine goodness and concern people had for a man with a tortured heart. I found that the more I exposed my wounds, without becoming a burden on those I exposed them to, the more I found an outstretched hand. Praise Jesus. May your reality be the same. I encourage you to seek out a priest, pastor, counselor, or friend. If you can give voice to your pain, you can begin to find relief from it. Please understand that some people are overwhelmed by the despair of others, but there are many who are not. Seek them out.

The shock one feels from divorce is something only those who have gone through it will understand. I had friends and family who went through divorce before me, and I really thought they could just get over it and move on. In fact, I wondered why they didn't. I couldn't relate to their pain as I never felt it myself. You may face this too.

I have since learned how precious genuine empathy can be. I have also discovered I can journey alongside a hurting person, whose pain I don't fully understand, without judging them for their feelings or the rate at which they are traveling. This is one of the many gifts that came from the refiner's fire of divorce. I can't help but wonder what gifts you will develop as you surrender to peace and happiness in the midst of turmoil. It will change you; allow it to be for the better.

Those who have not gone through divorce can only relate to it from the periphery. They can only relate to it by watching you go through it. They may see the devastation and havoc it wreaks, but they cannot know the extent of the physical, emotional, mental, and spiritual torture it causes. Do not despair that they do not understand fully what you are going through. You can find a way to work through the pain you are feeling. Be assured you *can* get through it. Do not give in to self-destructive coping strategies that come from trying to do it alone. I encourage you to begin by seeking help, first and foremost, from our Lord, Jesus Christ. I am not here to preach to you. I am only sharing my reality. My hope for you is that you emerge victorious from your divorce. I did, but I did it through a stronger relationship with God, which was further assisted through my attendance at a DivorceCare program. If you are unfamiliar with DivorceCare, then go to http://www.divorcecare. org/ to learn more about it. I strongly encourage you to get involved. Support is crucial when you are vulnerable.

When I speak of emerging victorious from your divorce, I am not talking about your divorce settlement. I am not talking about property or child custody. I speak only of emerging victorious in the spiritual battle you are now in. Make no mistake, you are in a spiritual battle, even if you are not a spiritual or religious person. The devil had my heart in his hand. He looked me in the eye and dared me to find peace and leave my anger behind. He told me, not directly but through temptation, that I must attack my spouse's character. He told me my hatred was justified. My decision to ignore evil and hatred affected my family, my children, my physical and spiritual health, and me as a whole forever. Yes, I took care of my children, my assets, and myself, but I also realized destroying another person means destroying another child of God as well as the mother of my children. You may not like what your spouse did to cause this situation. You probably have an immense dislike for them, but destruction is not the answer. My path to victory was only through forgiveness. I thank God my ex-wife chose the same path of civility I did. That was a blessing.

The devil stood in front of me every day and told me I should lash out at my wife. The devil tried to trip me up multiple times. The devil tried to make me feel and accept the pain of despair and loneliness. The devil tried to tell me I was worthless and washed up. I suspect the devil is attacking you as well. Divorce is evil. God despises divorce, but He does not despise divorced people. Do not fall victim to the temptation of causing your spouse pain. Do not fall into the trap of belittling your spouse in front of your children. Put your trust in God. Let Him help you. "Lord God, help me, please." Repeat the words. Believe He will help you and watch the glory of God begin to work in your life.

With regard to my divorce settlement, I will only say neither of us "won" nor came out "on top." The words of our mediator sum up the process we went through very well. She said, "It is obvious that neither of you wants to hurt the other." How you handle your divorce settlement is a choice. It is one of countless choices you get to make as you begin assuming control of your life and begin restoring order from the chaos. Divorce is, as I said, a psychic tsunami, and it leaves a mess of desolation in the end. The choices you make throughout the process will determine what you are left with when the storm finally ceases. The storm will end. Some people make good choices, and others make choices out of anger and mean-spiritedness. I encourage you to prayerfully consider the choices you are being confronted with. If all you leave behind is scorched earth, then rebuilding will take much longer.

The shock you feel does not cease rapidly. It doesn't go away as quickly as you would hope. The only way I knew how to defeat it was to get up each day with a longing for God's help, a belief He would help, and a promise to myself that I would try to be stronger that day than I was the day before. I recalled the children's song that says to "put one foot in front of the other .." That's all I could do. That's all

God asked me to do. That's all He asks any of us to do—to walk by faith one step and one day at a time. He handled the rest. I gave Him the opportunity to work in my life. I tried to visualize myself reaching up to the sky and God grabbing my hand to lift me to my feet. It may sound strange, but I did this day after day. There were days when I didn't feel like I could get up on my own without divine intervention. I eventually reached a point where I could get out of bed and begin the day without much effort, but I continued to be grateful to God for His loving assistance. Gratitude was yet another unexpected gift that began to develop in my character as a result of the refiner's fire of divorce.

I experienced new challenges every day. I saw people I thought were my friends only to realize they sided with my spouse rather than remain neutral. Likewise, people sided with me rather than remaining neutral. It may surprise you that I really didn't like it when people took either of our sides. I really didn't. I couldn't stand the thought of someone disliking my wife, estranged or not. As much as I hated it, I had to understand and accept it. I couldn't change it. My spouse's family lived all around me. My family was farther away and spread throughout the country. I didn't have much support locally other than a few good friends. The neutrality of her aunt and cousin was a blessing to me. My in-laws obviously had to side with their daughter. It was natural and fully acceptable. I held no ill will toward them. They were cordial to me and I to them. That meant a lot to me, as we had been very close. I loved them very much. I miss our regular interaction terribly. The loss of the relationship I had with my in-laws tore me apart. It was yet another shock I had to deal with.

I decided, very early in the separation, I would not use alliances to gain an upper hand. All I wanted was peace. If you understand that people will align with your spouse, you can deal with it like an adult and move forward with your life. Our situation was also difficult for the people around us. My approach to allegiances was to simply demonstrate I had no intention of destroying my spouse's character through the divorce process. Eventually, people began to see we could be near each other without spewing venom. I know it made my kids feel more at ease as well. They didn't get drawn into the devastating need to choose sides. They could continue to love us equally.

Shock was a constant part of my life during the initial stages of our separation. Grief became compounded grief, and loss became compounded loss—all of it led to living in a seemingly endless state of shock. The good news is it did end. I can't pinpoint when it happened, but I can tell you I no longer live with the surreal feeling brought about by shock and despair. School events and daily chores were more complicated. Almost everything I did stirred emotions. Things that used to be routine were no longer. They did, however, become easier and easier as a result of not isolating my ex through destructive behavior. I had to accept my new reality in life. Since I could not change it, I had to accept it and deal with it. This is the process of healing. It's not easy. It's not fun. It's hurtful at times, and sometimes you will just want to give up. Every time I felt weak, I simply talked out loud to God. I asked Him to help me. "Lord God, help me, please." I have lost track of the score between the devil and me, but I know God has helped me blow this game wide open. My soul shock has since become heavenly blessings.

Notes

Chapter 2

Managing Day to Day

I eventually realized I was spending too much time in my house alone. I was OK when my children were with me, but I hated it when they were not. I had to force myself to get out of the house, even just to go to the gas station and back. It was amazing how difficult it was for me to do simple tasks alone. Going to the grocery store was horrible. I felt like people could tell I was in the middle of a crisis. I was not thinking rationally, and my fear was much stronger than my confidence.

I remember going to the health food store to pick up Pink Lady apples on the Saturdays I didn't have my kids. It was a short trip from my house, but it became a liberating event. Today, looking back, I realize how totally devastated I was. I had to develop new routines little by little. I finally reached the point of being comfortable in my own skin. My message is to simply get out of the house and try to establish a new routine. Fear is a real part of adjusting from a married life to a single life. If you must, force yourself out of the house to do things as a single person. I had to get comfortable being single, and I hated it. I did it though. It was day to day, but I did it. Do not isolate yourself from the world.

Annual events, post separation, were tough as well. My brother has a big gathering each year for my nephew's birthday. I didn't want to go to it at first, but my children and I went anyway. Afterward, I was glad I went, but while I was there, people were, quite naturally, asking me where my wife was. I hated telling them we were separated. I hated to say the words, but I also hated it because people would get really somber afterward. We were at a party, and the last thing I wanted people to be was somber, especially when it was brought about by something I said.

This is part of life as a newly separated person. I call the new day-to-day experiences "The Firsts." As a single person, you have to grind through everything you normally did as a couple. Each of "The Firsts" can be an emotional event. Going to church, going to birthday parties, visiting family for the holidays, etc. will trigger emotion. As far as I can tell, this doesn't go away. I still find "emotional land mines" that trigger a deep emotional response. You may feel as though you are doing very well, and the next thing you know, you see a photo that reduces you to tears. I encourage you to cry because in so doing, you may discover you no longer cry as long or as intensely as you did in the beginning. I came to realize I had hours, days, if not entire weeks, I hadn't wept. I realized healing, at least a little, had begun in my life. And then, when I did hit a land mine, the best thing was to just let the tears come. It was, and continues to be, a grief that needs to be acknowledged and mourned. By acknowledging the loss of something I considered sacred and dear, I could move toward acceptance. I understand, from talking to other people who have been divorced much longer than me, this can happen many years following a divorce.

Notes

Chapter 3

Finding Peace

I was a Christian when I went through my separation and divorce. However, my faith had weakened a few years prior. I was not strong in faith. Maybe you are in a similar place. It really doesn't matter. Right now, as you read these words, you have the opportunity to accept Jesus Christ into your life. I was blessed with a quick realization that I was in crisis and that I needed help to carry on through this dark time in my life. I asked God to take me under His wing. I picked up the Bible and started to read it. I began to talk to God. I didn't really pray to Him, so to speak. I simply talked. I talked to Him about my feelings, my fears, my hopes, and my desires. It was a blessing. I encourage you to do the same. At one point, probably my lowest point, I was on the floor crying. I literally hit rock bottom. I didn't know how to carry on. God told me to stand and dry my eyes. So I did. My road to healing began at that very moment.

It's OK if you don't believe that the Lord told me what to do. I think you'll find that He will tell you what you need to do if you simply talk to Him. I later realized my actions at that moment were the first signs of strength after hitting rock bottom. It was the beginning of my healing. It was so powerful. Does this sound odd or unbelievable? All I can say is try it and let yourself heal rather than question it.

Finding peace while you are in the middle of divorce is not easy. It is possible though. I had to go through all the stages of grief just like you will. It is unhealthy to short-circuit the natural progression through denial, anger, bargaining, and depression to get to acceptance. You can reach acceptance fairly quickly though. It took me just over a year to progress through my initial shock to acceptance. I consider this to be fairly quick. In my opinion, the important part of healing is not getting stuck in any one of the stages of grief. Don't kid yourself either; once you get to acceptance, the road is still very difficult. It doesn't magically get better. Only time heals the wounds of divorce, but scars remain.

I also found journaling to be very therapeutic. It enabled me to express my thoughts so I could move on through the stages of healing. I didn't know I was moving forward as I wrote the words on the piece of paper. It wasn't until I went back, months later, and read my journal again that I could see the positive changes I was making. Additionally, some of what you've read so far is a direct result of my journaling years earlier. I was getting stronger, more confident, and happier. I had more to thank God for with each passing day. Even my handwriting improved over time, and my thoughts were more coherent. Journaling brought me peace. It enabled me to vent when I wanted to vent, and it enabled me to say what I wanted to say whenever I wanted to say it. I strongly encourage you to journal. Keep it private, but journal.

When I wrote, I talked to God and asked Him questions. I told Him how I felt. I asked Him for help. I even yelled at Him. Let Him know when you are mad, happy, fearful, or tired. Our God wants us to reach out to Him in our time of need. As you get your deepest thoughts out of your mind and onto the piece of paper, you relieve yourself of the built-up pressure caused by negativity.

Perhaps most importantly, I began to see a counselor to help me deal with my impending divorce. Actually, she was the one who encouraged me to journal. I found great comfort knowing I would have someone else I could talk to about my situation. Like journaling, I was able to solve challenges simply by talking about them. On a number of occasions, I would question the value of going to my counselor. After all, I felt I was the one who did most of the talking and my counselor simply listened. I eventually realized my counselor guided the conversations so I could come to the answers I needed to find. Sure enough, after a few months, I began to realize I was answering a lot of the questions I was raising. The voice of reason was coming out more with each visit. Eventually, I didn't need to talk to my counselor about my divorce any longer. I was handling my new life just fine. Talk to a counselor you feel comfortable with, talk to God always, and remember to repeat the words, "Lord God, help me, please."

It's important to realize that finding peace is different from finding happiness. It simply means you have reached a point in your life where you realize you can function on your own without your spouse. It also means you have quieted your heart. By this, I mean you have begun to approach life with a rational mind, and you are no longer focusing on hatred and fear. I found reading to be a major pathway to finding peace. I read the Bible as well as self-help books. Not being a big reader, it took me some time to finish reading the books I started. I wished there was a short book that would provide "hope fast." Unfortunately, there just didn't seem to be anything out there that provided what I was looking for. That too was an incentive for me to write the words you are now reading. There are plenty of incredibly good books on the subject of divorce, but I wasn't interested in curling up with a good three-hundred-plus-page book when I was in the middle of my own crisis. I wanted encouragement—fast—and that is what I hope you get from reading my story. Additionally, I listened to good music and frequently talked with good friends.

Finding peace, like everything else in the healing process, is about making good decisions. Decide right now that you will be OK. If, at any time, you have doubt in your heart, say the words, "Lord God, help me, please."

Notes

Chapter 4

Forgiveness

I found forgiveness to be the absolute most critical component of my healing process. It didn't come easily. I struggled with it at first but ultimately found it was the single most important action I made on my path to healing. The Bible makes it quite clear, if you cannot find forgiveness in your heart for another person, then God will not find you forgivable. Up to this point, I have not quoted the Bible in my writing, but reading the Bible was a huge part of my healing. I want to include the following Bible verse verbatim since this is such a critical component of moving forward in life after divorce.

Matthew 6:14–16, NIV

For if you forgive men when they sin against you, your heavenly Father will also forgive you. But if you do not forgive men their sins, your Father will not forgive your sins.

I could not get the words out of my mind after I read them. I realized I must forgive to be forgiven by my Lord. As a sinner, I knew I would always need God's forgiveness. Besides the fact that my God told me what I needed to do, forgiveness seemed logical, and it seemed like the right thing to do.

"I forgive her." I had to say those words over and over before it really sunk in. "I forgive her." In the end, I really did forgive my ex, and I seriously hope she forgives me for whatever it was that I did to contribute to the separation. After I forgave her, I began to feel the weight of the world lift from my shoulders. Life began to take on a new perspective. I was free to begin my new life, and I was free to move forward rather than wallow in pain and grief.

Forgiveness was the key that permitted me to enjoy the rest of my life. What happened in the past is no longer important. It's done. I couldn't change it, and I didn't control it. Yes, I still remember the pain, but I no longer let it consume me. Forgiveness does not require you to forget what you went through. It simply gives you the ability to move on with your life. Additionally, when you forgive your spouse, you set them free too.

I had a friend who held some resentment toward my ex-wife. He barely knew her. At one point, I had to explain to him where I was in my life regarding forgiveness. I had to explain to him I have forgiven her, and I harbor no bitterness toward my ex-wife. I think he was surprised that I was helping pack up some of her belongings she had left in the attic versus having her come and get them herself— or even throw them in the garbage. I explained I didn't seek to make her life hard. I genuinely wanted nothing in return other than to be left alone when my divorce was final. I didn't seek any battles, and I didn't want to win any wars. I just wanted peace in my life. Furthermore, I suggested he forgive too so he can find peace in his heart and so God can work in her life. I didn't hold anything against my ex-wife, and I explained I didn't need him to either.

I meant every word I told my friend. I was at peace, and all I wanted was peace. I would not wage a battle against my ex, and as a result, we have an amicable relationship. We do not talk frequently, but if we must, then it is easier than it would be if resentment and hatred persisted. More importantly, this is what my children see in their daily lives. Can you forgive? What if you do not forgive? I read the following in one of the daily DivorceCare e-mails: "If you do not forgive, you may get in the way of the work God is trying to do in the other person's life." That is something I did not want to be responsible for. I hope you too can find it in your heart to forgive. It could be the most important decision you make in your life as well as your ex-spouse's life. Forgiveness is hard, but the benefits are life-changing in a positive way.

Depending on where you are in the process of your separation or divorce, as well as the stages of grieving, this may not be possible for you right now. That's OK. Once you find peace, this will be possible. If you still can't find forgiveness in your heart, at least continue to say the words "I forgive her." Say it every day. Life will become magical once you truly believe the words you are speaking. I hope you can reach this point. It will change your life forever. I do not believe anyone will ever be ready to move into a future relationship until they truly forgive their ex as well as *themselves*.

In addition to forgiving my ex-wife, I also sought to reestablish an amicable relationship with my in-laws. I knew the relationship we once had was gone forever, but I wanted to make sure we could continue our lives with no ill will toward one another. I wrote to my in-laws and explained to them I had received the final divorce decree. It was a weird piece of mail to read because it was so informal and impersonal. I don't know what I really expected, but it wasn't what I received.

I wanted to write to my in-laws to, first and foremost, thank them for welcoming me into their lives over the past nineteen years. I also wanted to let them know I felt they were truly beautiful people, and I appreciated all the kindness they extended to me. I can honestly say my life was changed for the better through my interactions with them. I thanked my brother-in-law for his kindness. I always appreciated our philosophical conversations as well as our pointless, mundane exchanges about the trivialities of life. He challenged me to think outside of the box, and for that, I truly thanked him.

I wanted to share a piece of my heart with them, and I explained their daughter and sister would always hold a special place in my heart. True, I have had to learn to fall out of love with her, but I will always love her as a person and, more importantly, as the mother of our children. I explained I held no ill will toward her and prayed she held no ill will toward me. I believe that is the case.

Our relationship as spouses had come to an end, which is unfortunate. We did, however, work with each other in a peaceful manner, and neither of us looked to harm the other during the process of separation and divorce. As I stated earlier, neither of us came out of this situation "on top" or as the "winner." We did, however, treat each other respectfully and humanely. I am thankful to God for what we were able to accomplish. I explained we acted fairly, in alignment, and for the benefit of our children, and in that, I believe we succeeded. There are countless horror stories to the contrary, but again, it is a matter of choice.

Additionally, I thanked them for the love and devotion they have shown our children. Their stability through this rocky and confusing journey has made a positive impact on their lives. Our children are very blessed to have grandparents and an uncle like them in their lives.

Finally, I suggested that, as we go our separate ways in life from this point forward, I have a wish that all of us can face one another with open hearts, open minds, and perhaps even open arms. If this was wishing too much, I indicated that I respectfully understand. I let them know they still hold a special part of my heart, and I thank God for the blessings they have bestowed upon me.

I heard back from my in-laws after sending that letter. They were very open to carrying on a peaceful relationship. It would have been easy to simply write off my ex-wife's family as victims of our divorce. I didn't want to lose contact with them. We had a great relationship during the time I was married to their daughter, and there was no reason to let that relationship fade away.

What relationships can you restore? It's not necessarily easy, but forgiveness is well worth it in the end. I didn't want to be out in public and have to avoid people as a result of my divorce. Likewise, it would hurt me to see others avoiding me. Whoever the relationship is with, if it is worth saving, it may be up to you to save it. While I was not able to save my marriage, I was able to save some of the friendships I had when I was married.

I sincerely hope you can find it in your heart to forgive. I genuinely believe it is the most important act you will perform as you journey toward healing. Liberate yourself and experience the wonder of God's love in your life. Let God work in your life and let Him put you on a new path that will amaze you.

Notes

Chapter 5

New Beginnings

My ultimate victory came when I finally surmounted the doubt and fear I had about the future. I finally realized life wasn't as bad as it could have been, and while I did experience a significant traumatic event, I realized I would be able to recover and move forward in life. I entered a new phase of my life. It was a time of *new beginnings*. It took me just over a year to realize this. I hope you can reach a point of strength where you realize your goodness and value once again. I pray you can move forward in life as a healthy and new person. Put one foot in front of the other and continue to move forward. Nobody will make you successful in your post-divorce life other than you. Realize the goodness you have to offer and embrace it. By the same token, learn from your mistakes.

I realized, to avoid future failures in my relationships, I had to take inventory of my life and the events that led to my challenges. It wasn't comfortable looking back and reliving those events, but I took comfort in the fact that my reflection enabled me to see a clear difference between the man I was and the man I have become. I grew through the experience and pain. My reflection often revealed answers that didn't exist at the time I was crawling through them.

Yes, I did experience a terrible crisis in my life, one that I never thought would hit me. It was just one of those things that only happen to "other people"— separation and possible divorce. How did I end up in that situation? That was a question I asked myself repeatedly right after my wife told me she felt we should separate. My life was crushed.

Through this horrible crisis, I have learned a lot about myself. I've learned I'm not innocent or totally to blame. I blamed myself for a while and thought if I took the blame and fell on the proverbial sword, it would somehow bring my estranged wife back to me. However, that wasn't going to happen. I learned we hit a point in our relationship that is quite common for couples. I knew something was wrong, but I never knew exactly what it was. I had pressed my wife for answers. In the end, all she could say is she wanted a separation. It's sad, but it was my reality. The only question that remained was whether there was anything worth saving. I had my opinion. My wife had her opinion. We would see, in time, if our opinions were in sync or completely divergent. They were divergent.

When my world was rocked, I was forced to say goodbye to the only woman I've ever loved. I literally had to look her in the face and say goodbye. God, looking back on that day, I thought I was going to melt into the ground. I didn't know if I had anything left in me to pull myself up off the ground, let alone carry me from day to day.

The part that killed me the most was when she uttered the words "I'm done, it's over, I'm through." I wish I knew more about what was troubling her. Our situation might have been avoided if I did. Once my wife started to drift away, she found more comfort in other activities than in me. What a shame.

Through my crisis, I've learned a lot about myself. I've learned I needed to rededicate myself to my Lord. I've done that. I'm glad God has welcomed me back. I appreciate God's patience with me. He sent the Holy Spirit into my life once again. I'm alive! I'm reinvigorated. I'm excited about life again.

Additionally, I realized my life was out of balance. It's a fact. My spiritual life was waning, my mind was under-stimulated because of my perceived elevated levels of stress, my work dominated my thoughts and actions, and my health was in shambles. I've learned that mind, body, spirit, and career must be in balance to live a healthy life. I was out of whack.

Once I became more settled in my situation, I forced myself to read a number of books. Reading was not one of my desired hobbies, mostly because it takes me so long to actually read a book. However, reading did help me realize the possibilities that exist coming out of the flames that were once my marriage. I also learned it is possible to come out of separation with a stronger marriage than ever. I didn't control that possibility, and as such, I am divorced. Your results may be different.

When strengths and weaknesses are not clearly identified, terrible things happen inside a relationship. I can attest to it. Through this crisis, I've learned my strengths and weaknesses and have adjusted. Praise God. I feel good about my newfound strengths, and I know my weaknesses. I'm proud of my growth in this area. None of this would be possible if I didn't stretch or exercise my mind! I encourage you to read as much positive content as you can. *Brokenness and New Beginnings* is a lifeboat, so to speak, to quickly help you get to shore, steady your feet, and help you realize you have strength to stand up and begin walking once again.

It has been a while since I could stand tall. It has been a while since I was proud of my life or could even say that I love myself. It has been a while since I've been happy with my life. That's changing. God knocked me back to reality, grabbed me by the hand, and threw me on a new path of life. The path is rough. I climb over rocks and boulders each day. I dust off ash from the fires of pain.

Everything on this path is "new." I'm doing it, though, and so can you. It's day to day, but I'm doing it. Sometimes I cry. Sometimes I laugh. Sometimes I cheer myself on, but I have learned I can change. I've learned I don't always need to be right. I've learned that love is something to cherish every day versus taking it for granted. I've learned the value of a hug, a kiss, and the simple touch of a soft, loving hand. I've learned the value of the smell of perfume in my home and the value of a daily phone call from loved ones. I've learned the value of beautiful eyes. I've learned the value of change and the value of living in balance. I've learned the value of a prayer. I've learned the value of having my son see me cry versus trying to hide my feelings. I've learned the value of my kids seeing me pray. I've learned the value of family photos. I've learned the value of eating at a table with my family. Again, I've learned I can change. I've learned the value of my daughter saying she's proud of me. I've learned the value of humility. I've learned the value of being kicked so hard that you have to change your entire life. I've learned! I've learned the value of screaming, "I'm alive! I'm alive! I'm alive!" with the hopes of actually believing it one day. I've learned the value of every tear I have shed. I've learned the value of friends and the sorrow of not having more. I've learned the value of a flower. I've learned the value of people with heart, courage, and guts. I've learned the value of admitting when I'm wrong and trying to live life as a man of integrity. I've learned the value of having faith and repeatedly saying, "Yes, I can," while the devil continues to tell you you're worthless. I've learned the value of calling friends and having other men in my life willing to pray for me. I've learned the value of loyalty. I've learned the value of being humble without having to be humbled. I've learned the value of caring people and small social gatherings. I've learned the value of spending time with family during holidays, popping popcorn, and watching a movie. I've learned the value of having someone in your life you consider a confidant and lover. I've learned the value of getting knocked down and pulling yourself up again—all while you continually get beat by the evil of doubt and fear. I've learned the value of saying "I will" and believing today is a new day. I've learned the value of failing over and over and over again but having the guts to keep on trying. I've learned the value of a faith-filled mother and an honest father. I've learned the value of my brothers and my sister. And yes, I've learned I'm a better man today than I ever was before. Praise God Almighty!

I've also learned about sorrow, pain, sadness, loneliness, depression, fear, anger, hopelessness, agitation, defeat, and spiritual death. I've learned about the power and strength of evil. However, those evil things are weak once you realize the value of everything positive in your life. Evil can never penetrate the protective arm of Jesus Christ. They just can't! I no longer take anything for granted, especially a wonderful woman who actually encourages me to be my best. Life takes on new perspective when you sit at a kitchen table, post separation, without your spouse or children, and eat dinner alone. It makes you look in the mirror and analyze who you truly are. I have, and I no longer take anything for granted.

I have learned the goodness I bring to the world. I'm dedicated. I'm committed. I'm honest. I'm loyal. I'm a man of integrity. I'm passionate about the things important to me and now know what's actually important in life. I'll fight to make my wrongs right. I'll apologize. I'm a better man. I'm a better father. I'm a better employee. I'm a better boss. I have value. I have worth. I have something to offer the people in my life. I'm funny. I love. I care. I help. Most importantly, I'm a sinner, but I'm forgiven. Praise Jesus! Oh, praise You, Jesus!

Yes, today I'm a different man from who I ever was before. I have been torn down, stripped of everything I considered valuable, and have been rebuilt from the ground up by God Almighty. Life is good. God is great! I'm alive again. I live.

Today I praise God for the life He has given me. Divorce is evil. It's a plague on earth. However, I was able to remain true to my faith and keep my value system intact. I have, by the grace of God, kept my faith. It's stronger now than ever before. It has been a while!

I walk—I walk the path God told me to walk. God, I walk! I don't know where life will lead me. Pray that you emerge from the psychic tsunami called divorce as a better person. The scars of divorce will never fade, but the pain and suffering can. When you feel like you need help, reach your hands high into the air and imagine God helping you to your feet and say the words, "Lord God, help me, please." Give God and time a chance to help you realize all you value and all you now realize about yourself. You have value. You may feel brokenness as you read these words, but realize *new beginnings* await you.

Notes

Chapter 6

Relationship Transformations

I am happy to tell you that today I am living the next chapter of my life, and it is wonderful. No, everything isn't perfect. No, I didn't escape pain and challenge after my divorce, but I did meet a wonderful woman who saw the best in me, and today I am blessed to call Jennifer my wife.

I fully understand that it may be hard to read about my happiness and ability to move on with my life. I empathize with you and the pain you feel, but bear with me as I will definitely give you hope. If, up to this point, you have not yet realized my blessings were not man-made but rather blessings bestowed upon me by the Lord God, Jesus Christ, then let me tell you this is, indeed, the reality of my life.

I believe the words to follow will demonstrate how loving God is to those who fully submit to His mercy. I will share with you the speech I gave at my rehearsal dinner the day prior to our wedding. The words reveal my desire to remarry post divorce and God's power in times of relationship disaster. I believe it is assurance that through Him, all things are possible. If it is too early for you to read about this, then set the book down and pick it back up when you have more strength. Understand, however, that the blessings I share from this point forward are powerful and God-given. My message is that similar blessings are available to you too, but you must be willing to turn your life over to God and let Him work miracles through you. I pray that you may gain strength from my story, but I also understand that I've benefited from the gift of time. You may be simply wondering how you can just make it through today, let alone tomorrow. I understand this completely. Pause if you must. Bookmark this page and come back when you have the strength to do so. I promise—hope abounds. Remember: When you feel weak or vulnerable, always utter the words, "Lord God, help me, please!"

My Rehearsal Dinner Speech

I am really excited that we are all here tonight, and it's especially sweet to be sharing this time with friends and family. I wanted to take a few minutes—if you will indulge me—to share something with you. I hope I can make it through this without crying. But if I do cry, understand that they are tears of joy rather than sadness.

Psalms 20:1-9,NIV reads,

> [1]May the LORD answer you when you are in distress; may the name of the God of Jacob protect you. [2]May he send you help from the sanctuary and grant you support from

Zion. ³May he remember all your sacrifices and accept your burnt offerings. ⁴May he give you the desire of your heart and make all your plans succeed. ⁵May we shout for joy over your victory and lift up our banners in the name of our God.

May the LORD grant all your requests.

⁶Now this I know: The LORD gives victory to his anointed. He answers him from his heavenly sanctuary with the victorious power of his right hand. ⁷Some trust in chariots and some in horses, but we trust in the name of the LORD our God. ⁸They are brought to their knees and fall, but we rise up and stand firm. ⁹LORD, give victory to the king! Answer us when we call!

Today is a special day for obvious reasons. It is a day that I have been waiting for with much anticipation and with a burning desire. Today has a deeper meaning for me than the obvious, more than what you see before you. Today I celebrate a story that could only be made real through the blessings of God.

When I read the twentieth Psalm for the first time, it meant very little to me. However, when I came across it again, when I was at a different stage in my life, it spoke to me. I cried nearly every time I read it. Today Psalms 20, the Word of God, comes to life in our presence. Today, whether you realize it or not, we celebrate the victory of our Lord for He has answered me when I was in distress, He protected me from despair, He remembered my trust in Him, and He accepted my lowly praise. And in return, I have been blessed with the desire of my heart, and He has made all my plans succeed. Today my bride has agreed to give me her heart, and I have been blessed with her acceptance of mine. None of this would be possible without God working in my life over the past few years.

I stand before you today a very humbled man. The victory of which I speak is *not my* victory but rather

God's victory. For through me, the Lord has shown His compassion and healing power. The power of His right hand has been made known. He has answered my prayers from His heavenly sanctuary. The Lord has taken a once-brokenhearted man, raised him to his feet, pulled him out of the valley of death, accepted him into his fold once again, guided him down a new pathway in life, fed him, nourished him, strengthened him, and rebuilt him—entirely. Then the Lord placed a flower on my path—and she captured my heart the moment I saw her. What did I do to deserve such a beautiful woman as this?

Once again, let me read the words in the twentieth Psalm: "May he give you the desire of your heart and make all your plans succeed. May we shout for joy over your victory and lift up our banners in the name of our God."

As sure as I stand before you, I am raising my banner of praise to God for all to see. Today we celebrate *His* victory. Join me in raising our banners of praise and hold them high.

And if anyone of you holds sorrow in your heart, let today be a confirmation that the Lord God is alive and ready to achieve victory through you. Trust Him with all your worries and cares so that He may give you peace. And when He achieves victory through you, shout it out loud for all of us to hear, and I personally will raise my banner praising God just as high for you as the one you raise for Him today.

When I wrote this, I knew in my heart that through the grace of God, I would one day be sitting next to my bride-to-be here today. And I promised my Lord then that I would hold my banner, praising Him. So today I fulfill that promise, and today we see greatness prevail over despair, for the flower that was put on my path has taken me to *the garden* God promised I would one day see. Praise God, and thank you for being here with us, and thank you for letting me share this with all of you today!

Once all the heartache, sadness, and pain begin to fade into the recesses of your memory, and each day seems to be a little brighter than the previous, you can begin to experience the fruit of God's goodness in a very new and exciting way. After you have achieved your ultimate victory, you will be ready to move on with life and create a new beginning. Maybe you too will be able to offer hope to someone in crisis.

I have personally witnessed cases of people trying to fast-track their recovery to the "new beginnings" phase of life. However, this ultimately results in disaster. Unfulfilling, frequent, short-term physical relationships are one such example. However, much can be expected from your future if you are willing to let God walk you through the stages of healing.

The man I am today is much different from the man who started authoring this book. I am happily remarried and have a beautiful wife with whom I enjoy every day God allows me to have with her. We are products of similar divorce situations. It is because of the pain we each went through that we have a much stronger and healthier respect for each other.

You too can reach this point in your life if you so desire. Ultimately, I am at this point in my life because I followed God, listened to Him, and let Him guide me through the darkest point in life. Will you allow God to work in your life? I suggest you not harbor hatred for your ex-spouse. It will only wear you down and elongate the pain you feel. Quite honestly, your hatred toward your ex doesn't hurt them in the least. In fact, they probably expect it. They have "moved on" in life, and now it's time for you to do the same. If you cannot change the state of your failed marriage, then you must move on with your life.

The process of becoming a "new you" will not be easy. Some of my relationships with relatives faded, some actually went from good to bad, and surprisingly, others actually improved. My relationship with my ex-wife's parents went from neutral to nonexistent. I'm not sure why, but it did. I've wanted to maintain an amicable relationship, one that simply made the inevitable periodic run-in bearable and comfortable rather than awkward. The friendly wave as we passed each other's home seemed to fade. It seemed they did not care to acknowledge me regardless of whether I was alone or with my kids. In my mind, a simple wave would produce goodwill and perhaps even a smile from their grandchildren. I like to assume they did not see us, but I will continue to wave whenever we pass by one another. The bottom line is that you cannot expect every aspect of every relationship to be a bed of roses. It's good to want it, but you have no control over other people's actions.

I did experience situations that cut me to the core of my being. I've been stunned by certain people's actions. I recall a time when Jennifer and I saw ex-relatives while we were shopping in a store. Their child did not understand how divorce works. She still referred to me as her brother-in-law. She got excited when she saw us. She waved and exclaimed, "It's my brother-in-law!" Her father guided her down the aisle, explaining, "He's not your brother-in-law." She was more than likely confused and saddened by the interaction than anything else. A simple wave, smile, and amicable interaction was what I had hoped for, but it was not to be. I'm not in any way implying that these are bad people. Their relationship with my ex-wife and her new husband has developed and evolved over time. There is truly no reason to maintain an active relationship with me. The bottom line is do your part to keep things amicable and realize that your effort may not be reciprocated.

My ex-wife's aunt, cousin and her husband, and her brother have always treated me and Jennifer extremely well. They still do. When my ex-brother-in-law is in town, and I'm outside my house, he will stop, get out of his car, shake my hand, and have a pleasant conversation. We even received a Christmas card this past year. It was the first in twelve years, and it actually made me very happy. I was happy to tell my children their uncle had sent us a card. It showed them, perhaps indirectly, that peace can shine through the ashes of a failed marriage.

I share these interactions with you in an effort to help you understand how relationships change over time. That change can be painful though. Likewise, you will quickly understand who your faithful friends are as you traverse your new life. You may not be able to save every relationship, but you will surely cherish the ones you do.

Looking back, I believe my nonconfrontational stand with my ex-wife paid dividends. I do not believe the relationships I have today with her family members would have survived had I gone on the attack. I would likely not have gained anything by disparaging her, but I surely gained a lot by being kind, even when it was hard to do so.

Notes

Chapter 7

Moving On

It was only after I achieved my ultimate victory that I could even think about a new relationship. I recall my daughter suggesting I "get out there and meet someone." God bless her. She wanted me to be happy. However, for me, I was married until the point in time when the divorce was final. I would not go on any date prior to receiving the documentation finalizing my divorce. That day did arrive, and I was nervous about meeting someone new. The process of asking someone on a date was never something I was particularly good at. I obviously can do it, but I was always nervous to the point of nausea when it came time to act.

I avoided the subject of dating for a while and simply consumed my free time playing games online. This seemed to be an acceptable way to "get through" the day—that is, right up to the point when my mother told me, "Get off the computer and go meet someone, for goodness sake!" God bless her. Sometimes I need a good, blunt proverbial slap upside the head to take action. At the time, it wasn't so funny, but I laugh every time I look back at that conversation; and now Jennifer can laugh at it too.

I was fortunate enough to have my daughter help me pick out some new "up-to- date" clothing. I didn't see the need for it at the time, but I did, eventually, realize how correct she was. I got professional photos taken for my eventual online profile. Needless to say, out of about a hundred pictures, I only found three potential photos that didn't make me cringe.

I was still unsure of myself, and the thought of "advertising" my availability was foreign to me. However, I knew I didn't want to spend the rest of my days as a single man, so I had to make an effort to meet people. I personally enjoyed being married and wanted someone to share my life with. You may feel otherwise, and that is perfectly acceptable. Read *It's Okay to Be Single* by Heather Marie Edmund, Westbow Press. I suggest you be true to yourself and don't let anyone pressure you into doing something you do not want to do.

I was fortunate enough to only meet one person who had vastly different views relative to dating before meeting my now wife. The second person I met online is now my wife, and we'll be celebrating eleven years of marriage this year.

The fact that Jennifer went through a remarkably similar divorce as I did made for some interesting conversations early in our relationship. We held everything close to our chest and were overly cautious about opening up to each other. We also had concerns about how to protect what little assets we each had. Our past failed relationships caused us to fear losing what we had should our new relationship fail. We had some very honest and open dialogue on the subject before we felt comfortable relaxing in our own relationship. You may have similar feelings as you begin to enter the next stage of your life. You need to do what is right for you. For us, however, we reached a point where we felt the need to be natural in our relationship and trust that we would not be hurt. In a way, it was the act of being vulnerable that strengthened our relationship.

It is possible to trust once again. It's difficult. It is my opinion that the reason so many second marriages fail is because of the fact that there is at least one person holding on to something from the past or trying to protect something from possible loss. We jointly decided that neither of us could live in such a relationship, let alone a marriage.

I enjoyed being married, and I am a family-oriented person, and while I did not lose my children, the mere thought of "shared custody" tore my heart apart. Even fifty-fifty custody is a loss. Nobody likes being lonely. I could handle being alone, but without my children and a loving relationship, I felt empty. Though I managed to deal with the hand I was dealt, I did know I wanted to remarry. Shortly after Jennifer and I started dating, I asked her if she ever saw herself being married again. When she indicated she did not, I asked her what we were doing dating each other if there was no ultimate destination. It was a bold question and statement on my part. The reality of the situation is that she was dealing with her own challenges and fears associated with our new relationship. She too was protecting herself from potential pain and disappointment. Would I hurt her the way her ex did? Should you enter into a new relationship, post divorce, it is important to be aware of the challenges your partner is dealing with. Be patient, but also be transparent. Talk about the feelings and concerns you have. If you cannot be open and honest, then I would suggest that you are only setting yourself up for another failed relationship.

Notes

Chapter 8

Fight Fair

I was never used to fighting in my first marriage. When Jennifer and I got into our first argument, I didn't know how to react. I wanted to retreat. However, she said something that stuck with me to this day. She said, "If I didn't love you or care, then I wouldn't say anything at all." Wow. That was another proverbial smack in the head. I realized "peace" does not necessarily equate with "good marriages." When we care for someone or something so deeply, and it's challenged, then we have a reaction that is often heated. I had to get used to this as it was foreign to me. I had to realize that so long as we "fight fair" we'll remain on a solid foundation. Once we begin to hurt the other person through personal insults or belittling words, we cross the line and enter into the "unfair fight" zone. Arguing is natural in marriage, so I've learned; however, emotionally hurting your spouse, belittling your spouse, or physically hurting your spouse is not.

You can find happiness if you are willing to open up to another person. If you are willing to subject yourself to the potential pain and discomfort of an ill-fated relationship, you just might find the love of your life. If you avoid healthy disagreement in the hopes of maintaining peace, then you risk the opportunity to be free with your thoughts and points of view. I have learned this is unhealthy. If you put up a façade to protect yourself from potential pain, I'd suggest you're not yet ready for a new relationship. I'm not a counselor or relationship expert though.

That said, I found I could "be me" and have someone love me the way I am. That is very liberating.

We often use our past as learning experiences, and it's quite natural to want to protect ourselves from harm. I often think of the manner in which Jesus taught his disciples. He would often use parables or contradictions to make His point; examples are "The first shall be last and the last shall be first," "The rich shall be poor and the poor shall be rich," etc. In many ways, opening yourself up to pain and making yourself vulnerable is the way to finding the true love you deserve. It also requires that you fully understand whether the person you are with believes the same.

Notes

Chapter 9

Where from Here?

Where from here? That is the ultimate question. Where will you go from this point to live a productive and fruitful life? Will you move on with your life, or will you focus on the past pain and turmoil? I decided to focus on the future. It was important for me to forgive and move forward. I prayed for God to get me to the point where I could carry myself through each day, and He answered my prayers.

You can experience happiness once again. You can experience love again. If I can do it, then I know you can too. Consideration of a new relationship may be foreign to you at this stage in your life. My message is, as it has been throughout this book, anything is possible through God. He stands ready to help you through the most challenging time of your life. Open up your heart and ask Him to come in and heal you from the inside out. Submit to His mercy and watch how wonderful your life can be.

I've referenced my "kitchen table" event a number of times so far because it was so painful, and it hurt me badly, but I remember the first time I sat at my kitchen table alone, as a newly single man facing the sting of divorce. I remember the lump in my throat, the pain I felt, and the drool dripping from my mouth as I cried. I had my food in front of me, but I couldn't stomach eating it. I felt like a broken man without purpose—wondering what my children were doing as I sat alone at my kitchen table. It was surreal. It was horrible and dark. Evil had raised its head and spit in my face, but I managed to make it through that dinner and that day. God's grace enabled me to make it through that day. I am thankful for His blessing.

You may have your own vivid memory of a particularly painful day or event. Your path today may appear to be ash, burned earth, and lifeless; however, keep walking in faith, and you will eventually see green amid the black and gray. That glimmer of life is your strength. Grab onto it and keep putting one foot in front of the other. If you can save your marriage, then do so. If, like me, that choice is not one you control, then trust in God. Maintaining a willingness to grind through the low points in your life can lead to brighter days ahead.

I am not a doctor or a psychiatrist. I am not a psychologist or a sociologist. I am not a theologian or a religious educator. I am not a professional writer or a master storyteller. I am simply a humbled man who has survived separation and divorce, and I pray I have offered you a story of hope.

I am a humbled man. Praise Jesus.

Lord God, help me, please.

Notes

Acknowledgments

I would like to thank the following people for helping me through the challenges of life caused by the devastation of divorce:

- My wife Jennifer for allowing me to be myself, for encouraging me to pursue writing this book, and for loving me always.
- Ann Jacobs for her thoughtful feedback and advice on my initial manuscript.
- Steve Larsen for being a friend through every step of my journey through divorce and beyond.
- Thomas Kesselring for being the voice of reason and a guide during my dark days of separation and divorce.

- Grace Covenant Church for running the DivorceCare program that ultimately helped me move forward in life.
- Jesus Christ for allowing me to call on Him for help—more times than anyone could ever imagine—and for His desire to have me call on Him even more.

Printed in the United States
by Baker & Taylor Publisher Services